COLLECTIONS

A Harcourt Reading / Language Arts Program

*Come on! New
friends are waiting
to meet you!*

COLLECTIONS

A Harcourt Reading / Language Arts Program

TOGETHER AGAIN

SENIOR AUTHORS

Roger C. Farr • Dorothy S. Strickland

AUTHORS

Richard F. Abrahamson • Alma Flor Ada • Bernice E. Cullinan • Margaret McKeown • Nancy Roser
Patricia Smith • Judy Wallis • Junko Yokota • Hallie Kay Yopp

SENIOR CONSULTANT

Asa G. Hilliard III

CONSULTANTS

Karen S. Kupiter • David A. Monti • Angelina Olivares

⧉Harcourt

Orlando   Boston   Dallas   Chicago   San Diego

Visit *The Learning Site!*
www.harcourtschool.com

ISBN 0-15-317799-3

1 2 3 4 5 6 7 8 9 10   048   2003 2002 2001 2000

Dear Reader,

  In **Together Again**, there are lots of friends to meet. First, you will go to a special party. Then you will meet some children just like you who can do many things. Last, you will meet some animals that find out how important it is to work together. Come on and join the fun!

Sincerely,

The Authors

The Authors

Look at Me Now

Contents

Just for Fun

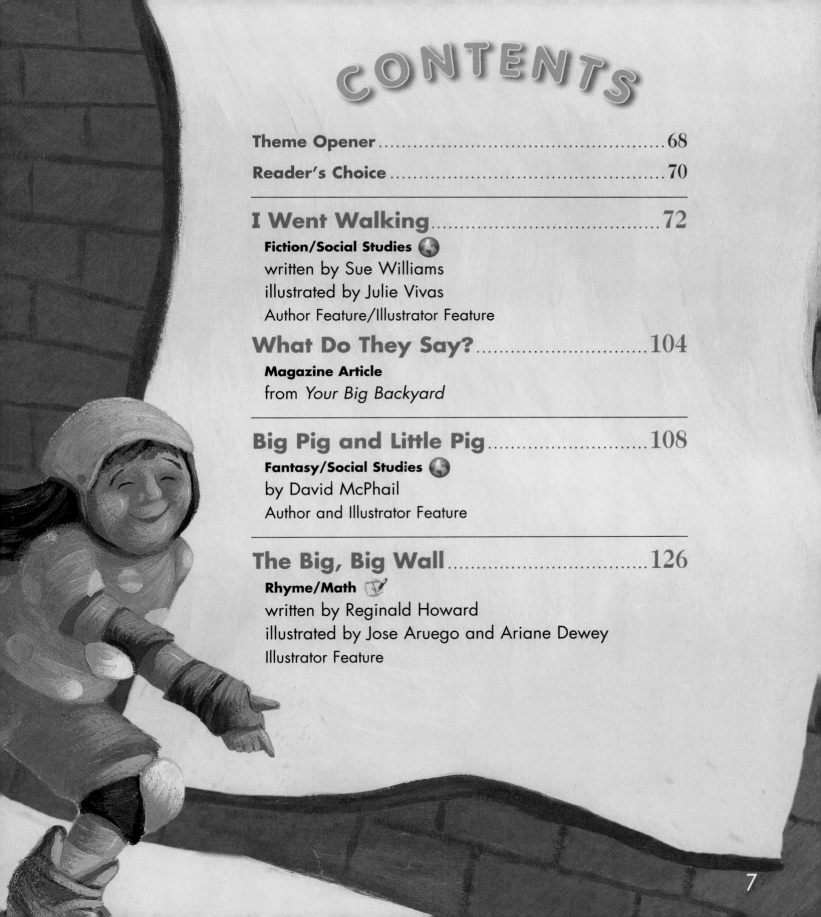

CONTENTS

Theme

Look at Me Now

8

Reader's Choice

Have You Seen My Cat?
by Eric Carle

A boy meets many different cats
before he finds his own.

Award-Winning Author
FROM THE LIBRARY

Have you seen my cat?
Eric Carle

Do Monkeys Tweet?
by Melanie Walsh

Find out what kinds of sounds different animals make.

Award-Winning Author

Who Am I?
by Nancy Christensen

Who am I? Read to find out who is the mystery animal.

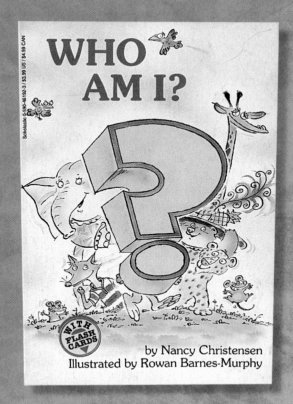

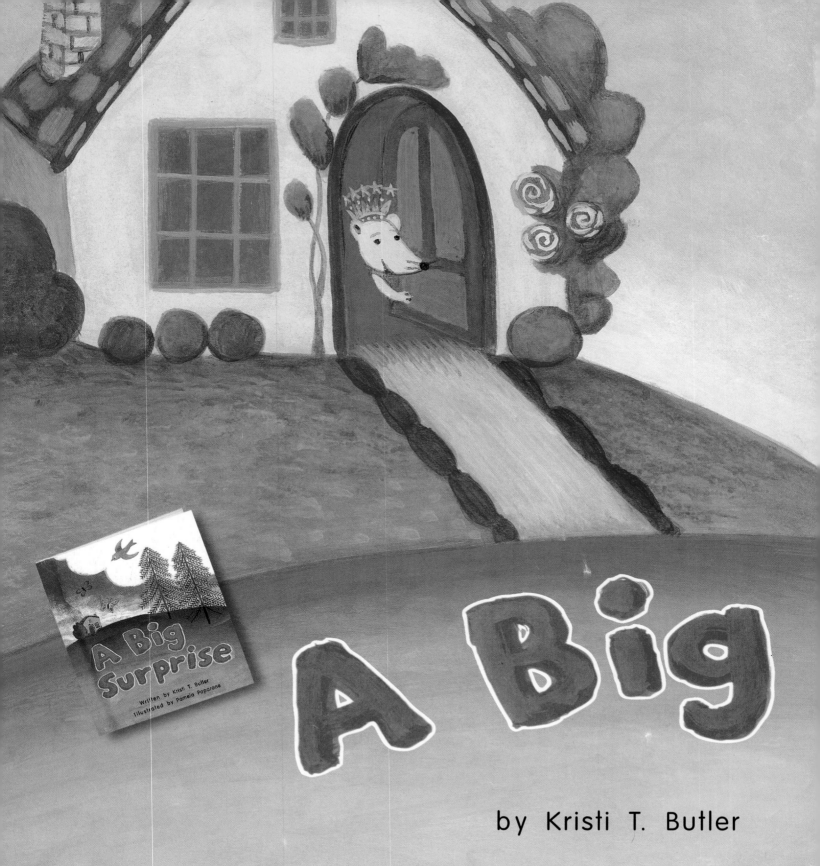

A Big Surprise

Written by Kristi T. Butler
Illustrated by Pamela Paparone

A Big

by Kristi T. Butler

Surprise

illustrated by Pamela Paparone

Here is the dog.

Here is the frog.

Here is the cat.

Here is the hat.

Here is the fox.

Here is the box.

Here is the house.

Here is the mouse.

Here is the snake.

Here is the cake.

What a big surprise!

25

Pam Paparone

Pam Paparone loves to celebrate her birthday. One year she gave herself a birthday party! There was a big cake and lots of dancing.

Pam Paparone thought of this birthday party when she began drawing the pictures for A Big Surprise. She wanted to make sure that Mouse s party had all the decorations and goodies she had.

Pam Paparone

Visit *The Learning Site!*
www.harcourtschool.com

27

Happy Birthday

written by Alan Benjamin
illustrated by Mary Grand Pré

Have a wonderful birthday,
a day full of cheer,
and when the day's done,
have a wonderful year.

Make a birthday card for Mouse.

30

Fold a sheet of paper in half.

Write "Happy Birthday, Mouse!" on the front of the card.

Write your name on the inside of the card.

Come here, Tiger.

Where is that cat?

Is that cat in the bed?

Come here, Tiger.

Is that cat in the box?

Come here, Tiger.

Is that cat in the tub?

Come here, Tiger.

Is that cat in the hat?

Come here, Tiger.

Where are you, Tiger?

Look! Here you are!

Meet the Author/Illustrator

Lisa Campbell Ernst

Lisa Campbell Ernst loves to write books about animals. Before she wrote "Come Here, Tiger," she thought about her own pets.

They became the models for the animals in the story. Lisa Campbell Ernst's daughter became the model for the girl who is looking for Tiger!

Lisa Campbell Ernst

Visit *The Learning Site!*
www.harcourtschool.com

46

RESPONSE ACTIVITY

Oh Where, Oh Where Has My Little Cat Gone?

The girl in the story looked all over for her cat, Tiger. Sing "Oh Where, Oh Where Has My Little Dog Gone?" Use the word **cat** instead of **dog**.

Oh where, oh where has my little cat gone?
Oh where, oh where can he be?
With his ears cut short and his tail cut long,
Oh where, oh where can he be?

Look at Me

by
Margaret Matthews

photography by
Shelley Rotner

It used to be hard to talk.

Look at me now.

It used to be hard to run.

Look at me now.

It used to be hard to hop.

Look at me now.

It used to be hard to paint.

Look at me now.

It used to be hard to read.

Look at me now.

We are good at
lots of things now.

We bet you are, too!

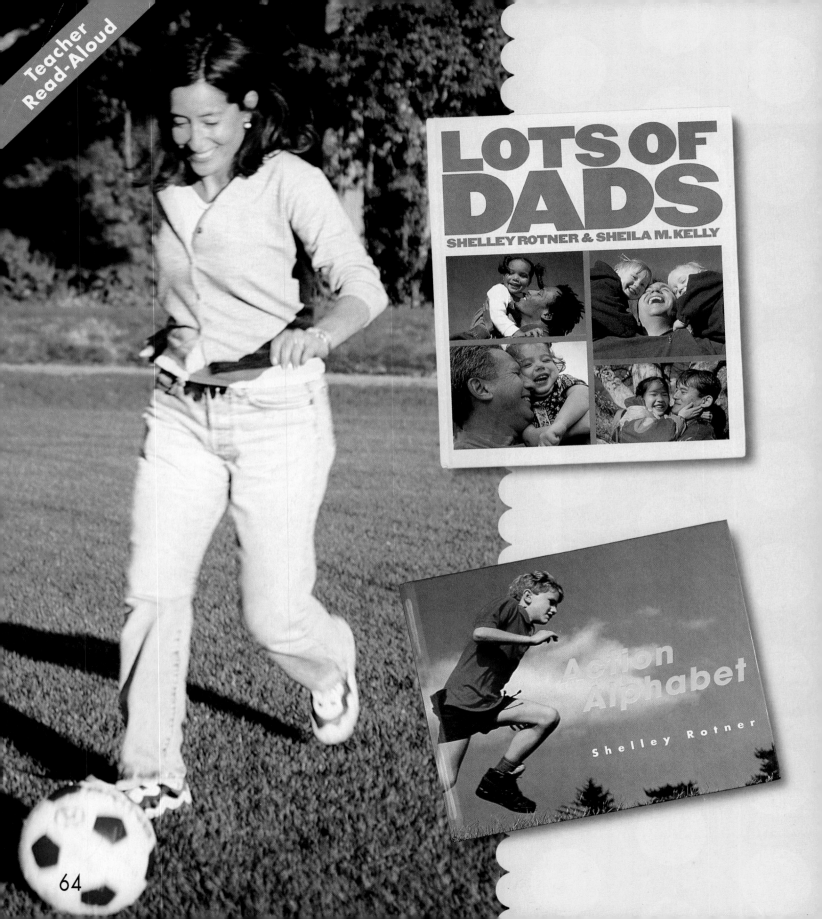

LOTS OF DADS

SHELLEY ROTNER & SHEILA M. KELLY

Action Alphabet

Shelley Rotner

64

Meet the Photographer

Shelley Rotner

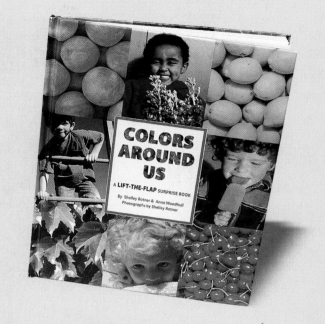

Shelley Rotner lives in Massachusetts, but she loves to travel. When she visits new places with her husband and daughter, she always takes her camera. Shelley Rotner snaps pictures of the people, animals, and sights she wants to remember and share with others. For "Look at Me," she took photographs of children in many different cities.

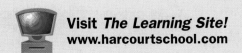

Visit *The Learning Site!*
www.harcourtschool.com

65

I Can Do It Mobiles

I can write.

I can draw.

Make a mobile.

Share things you can do now

that you are in first grade.

1. On paper circles, write new things you can do now.

2. On the back of each circle, draw a picture to go with your sentence.

3. Use yarn and tape to hang your circles from the hanger.

67

Just for Fun

Reader's Choice

Happy Birthday

by Tami Butler

Duck and Pig enjoy celebrating
their birthdays together.

FROM THE LIBRARY

We Play on a Rainy Day

by Angela Shelf Medearis

Children have fun playing together in the sun and in the rain.

Award-Winning Author

My Friends

by Taro Gomi

A girl talks about the many things she has learned from her friends.

ALA Notable
Book

I Went Walking

WRITTEN BY
Sue Williams

ILLUSTRATED BY
Julie Vivas

I Went

Walking

WRITTEN BY
Sue Williams

ILLUSTRATED BY
Julie Vivas

I went walking.

What did you see?

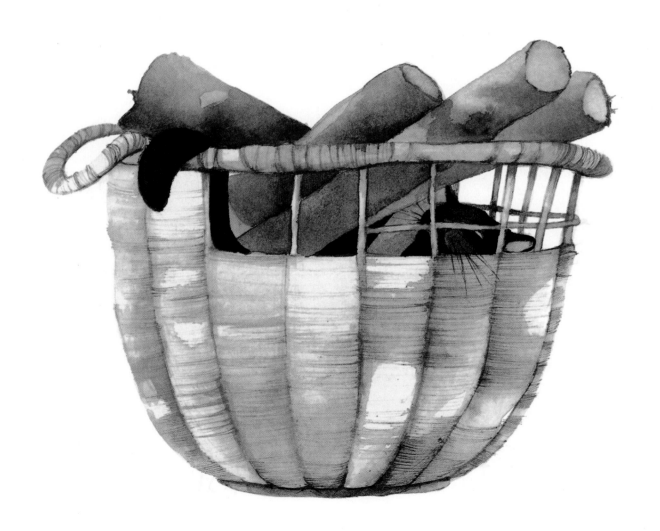

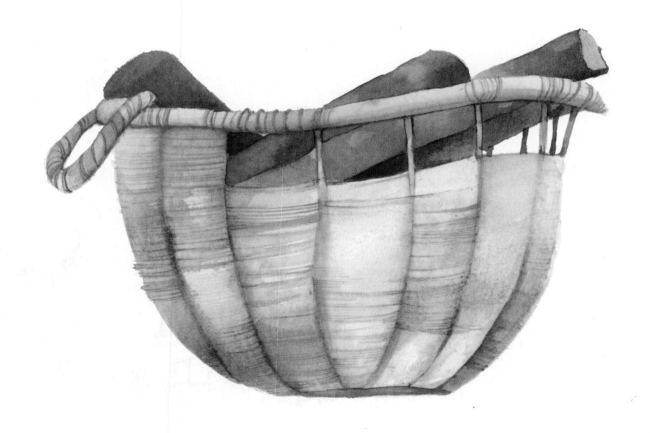

I saw a black cat
Looking at me.

I went walking.

What did you see?

I saw a brown horse
Looking at me.

I went walking.

What did you see?

I saw a red cow
Looking at me.

I went walking.

What did you see?

I saw a green duck
Looking at me.

I went walking.

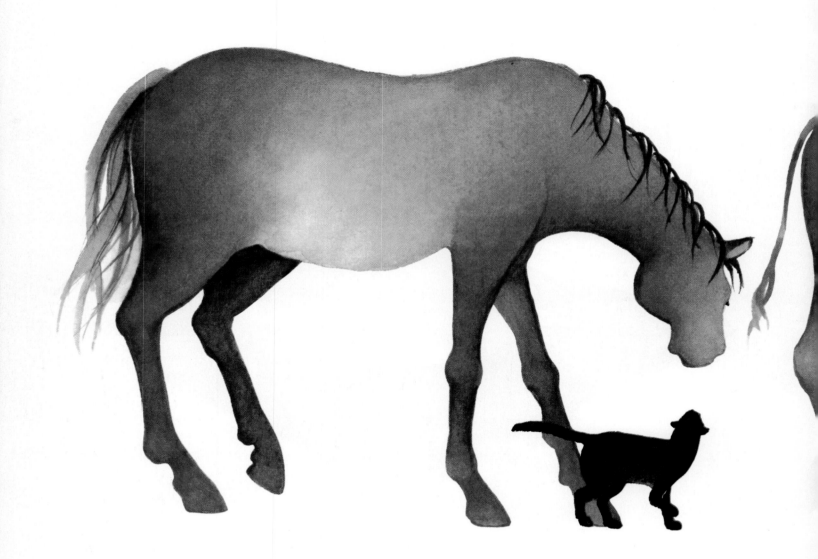

What did you see?

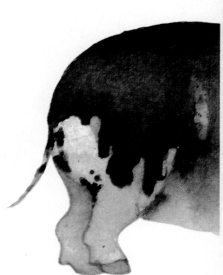

I saw a pink pig
Looking at me.

I went walking.

What did you see?

I saw a yellow dog
Looking at me.

I went walking.

What did you see?

100

I saw a lot of animals
Following me!

Sue Williams

When Sue Williams wrote "I Went Walking," she lived on a farm in the hills of Adelaide, Australia. On cold winter mornings, she had to break the ice on the troughs so her animals could drink. When the animals saw her, they followed her, just as the animals in the story follow the boy!

Meet the Illustrator

Julie Vivas

Julie Vivas likes to go for long walks. While she is walking, she often stops and sketches the people she sees. When she starts a new book, she looks through her sketches. She often finds one that would fit in the story. The little boy in "I Went Walking" came from a sketch of a child who lived in her neighborhood.

Quack,
quack.

This is a duck.

What Do

Moo-o-o-o.

This is a cow.

104

Hee-haw, hee-haw.

This is a donkey.

They Say?

Gobble, gobble.

This is a turkey.

Follow the Animals

Play animal follow-the-leader.

1. Choose an animal and draw it.

2. Be the leader.
   Say the rhyme and
   move like your animal.

106

A little duck went out to play.
Back and forth it moved
this way.

Come along and follow me,

A little duck is what you'll be!

by David McPhail

"I am hot," said Big Pig.

"Me, too," said Little Pig.

"I am going to make a pool,"
said Big Pig.

"Me, too," said Little Pig.

"I am going to dig a hole,"
said Big Pig.

"Me, too," said Little Pig.

"I am going to get a bucket,"
said Big Pig.

"Me, too," said Little Pig.

"I am going to fill up the pool," said Big Pig.

"Me, too," said Little Pig.

"Now I can sit back down,"
said Big Pig.

"Me, too!" said Little Pig.

Meet the Author
David McPhail

David McPhail loves to draw pigs. When he was a child, his favorite character was the pig Wilbur, in the book <u>Charlotte's Web</u>. "Pigs tickle me," he says. "They're fun because they do such silly things!" He hopes you giggled when you read "Big Pig and Little Pig"!

David McPhail

Visit *The Learning Site!*
www.harcourtschool.com

122

123

Let's Dig In!

Make Big Pig's favorite snack.

YOU WILL NEED

1. Cut circles with cookie cutters in your bread.

2. Spread strawberry jam on the big circle.

3. Cut one of the little circles in half.

4. Make a pig face. Use raisins for eyes and nostrils.

Write a sentence about
your favorite snack.
Share your sentence
with classmates.

I like
apples.

125

by Reginald Howard • illustrated by Jose Aruego and Ariane Dewey

The Big, Big Wall

Award-Winning Author/Illustrators

The Big, B

ig Wall

Humpty Dumpty
sat on a wall.

He did not want to
have a big fall.

One friend came
to the big, big wall.

"I will help you.
You will not fall."

"Oh, not you.
You look too small."

Two friends came to
the big, big wall.

"We will help you.
You will not fall."

"Oh, not you.
You look too small."

Three friends came
to the big, big wall.

"We will all come together.
You will not fall."

Humpty Dumpty
smiled at his friends.

"Now I will come
back down again."

Meet the Illustrators

Jose Aruego

Jose Aruego had a pet pig when he was young. "I loved that pig! He was so soft and funny." When Jose Aruego had to find a way to keep Humpty Dumpty from having a great fall, he thought about his pig, Snort. He decided that a pig would be a great cushion for Humpty Dumpty!

Ariane Dewey

Ariane Dewey has lots of rabbits visit her yard. She loves to watch them nibble dandelions. Ariane Dewey thought about those rabbits as she painted the rabbit in "The Big, Big Wall." She says that cheery colors make her feel good. She hopes her purple rabbit and colorful animals make you happy, too.

Visit *The Learning Site!*
www.harcourtschool.com

141

RESPONSE ACTIVITY

Walk With Me

Humpty Dumpty's friends worked together to help him get down from the wall. Work together with a partner in this game.

1. Stand beside your partner.

2. Tie one of your legs to one of your partner s legs.

3. Try walking or hopping.

Share with classmates what happens.
What did you learn about working together?

Acknowledgments

For permission to reprint copyrighted material, grateful acknowledgment is made to the following sources:

Atheneum Books for Young Readers, an imprint of Simon & Schuster Children's Publishing Division: Cover photograph from *Action Alphabet* by Shelley Rotner. Copyright © 1996 by Shelley Rotner.

Candlewick Press, Inc., Cambridge, MA: Cover illustration from *flower in the garden* by Lucy Cousins. Copyright © 1992 by Lucy Cousins.

Chronicle Books: Cover illustration from *My Friends* by Taro Gomi. Copyright © 1989 by Taro Gomi.

Dial Books for Young Readers, a division of Penguin Putnam Inc.: Cover photographs by Shelley Rotner from *Lots of Dads* by Shelley Rotner and Sheila M. Kelly. Photographs copyright © 1997 by Shelley Rotner.

Dutton Children's Books, a division of Penguin Putnam Inc.: Cover illustration from *Emma's Pet* by David McPhail. Copyright © 1985 by David McPhail. Cover illustration from *Pigs Ahoy!* by David McPhail. Copyright © 1995 by David McPhail.

Greenwillow Books, a division of William Morrow & Company, Inc.: Cover illustration by Jose Aruego and Ariane Dewey from *Come Out and Play, Little Mouse* by Robert Kraus. Illustration copyright © 1987 by Jose Aruego and Ariane Dewey. Cover illustration by Jose Aruego and Ariane Dewey from *Dance Away* by George Shannon. Illustration copyright © 1982 by Jose Aruego and Ariane Dewey. Cover illustration by Jose Aruego and Ariane Dewey from *Lizard's Song* by George Shannon. Illustration copyright © 1981 by Jose Aruego and Ariane Dewey.

Harcourt, Inc.: I Went Walking by Sue Williams, illustrated by Julie Vivas. Text copyright © 1989 by Sue Williams; illustrations copyright © 1989 by Julie Vivas.

Houghton Mifflin Company: Cover illustration from *Do Monkeys Tweet?* by Melanie Walsh. Copyright © 1997 by Melanie Walsh.

Little, Brown and Company (Inc.): Cover illustration from *First Flight* by David McPhail. Copyright © 1987 by David McPhail.

Little Simon, an imprint of Simon & Schuster Children's Publishing Division: Cover photographs by Shelley Rotner from *Colors Around Us* by Shelley Rotner and Anne Woodhull. Photographs copyright © 1996 by Shelley Rotner.

William Morrow & Company, Inc.: "Happy Birthday" from *A Nickel Buys A Rhyme* by Alan Benjamin. Text copyright © 1993 by Alan Benjamin.

National Wildlife Federation: "What do they say?" from *Your Big Backyard* Magazine, July 1996. Text copyright 1996 by the National Wildlife Federation.

North-South Books. Inc., New York: Cover illustration by Pamela Paparone from *Ten Dogs in the Window* by Claire Masurel. Illustration copyright © 1997 by Pamela Paparone. Cover illustration from *Five Little Ducks* by Pamela Paparone. Illustration copyright © 1995 by Pamela Paparone.

Scholastic Inc.: Cover illustration by Rowan Barnes-Murphy from *Who Am I?* by Nancy Christensen. Illustration copyright © 1993 by Nancy Hall, Inc. A *Hello Reader!* published by Cartwheel Books, a division of Scholastic Inc. Cover illustration by Sylvia Walker from *We Play on a Rainy Day* by Angela Shelf Medearis. Illustration copyright © 1995 by Sylvia Walker. A *Hello Reader!* published by Cartwheel Books, a division of Scholastic Inc. Hello Reader! and Cartwheel Books are registered trademarks of Scholastic Inc.

Simon & Schuster Books for Young Readers, an imprint of Simon & Schuster Children's Publishing Division: Cover illustration from *Have You Seen My Cat?* by Eric Carle. Copyright © 1987 by Eric Carle Corp. Cover illustration from *Ginger Jumps* by Lisa Campbell Ernst. Copyright © 1990 by Lisa Campbell Ernst. Cover illustration from *Duke the Dairy Delight Dog* by Lisa Campbell Ernst. Copyright © 1996 by Lisa Campbell Ernst. Cover illustration from *Bubba and Trixie* by Lisa Campbell Ernst. Copyright © 1997 by Lisa Campbell Ernst. Cover illustration by Jose Aruego and Ariane Dewey from *Herman the Helper* by Robert Kraus. Illustration copyright © 1974 by Jose Aruego and Ariane Dewey. Cover illustration by Pam Paparone from *Fire Fighters* by Norma Simon. Illustration copyright © 1995 by Pam Paparone.

Photo Credits

Key: (T)=top, (B)=bottom, (C)=center, (L)=left, (R)=right
Page 26, Sal DiMarco/Black Star; 31, Hot Shots Imaging; 47 Vedros & Associates; 48, 49, Hot Shots Imaging; 64, Impress, Inc.; 66, 67, Hot Shots Imaging; 102, Robert Weaverling / Pro-Lab Photography; 103, Nancy Cohen / Black Star; 104(t) John Shaw; 104(b) Peter Cade / Tony Stone Images; 105(t) Lynn Stone; 105(b) Jack Daniels / Tony Stone Images; 106, Hot Shots Imaging; 123, Rick Friedman/ Black Star; 124, 125, Hot Shots Imaging; 141, Lisa Quinones / Black Star; 143, Hot Shots Imaging. Tabletop photography by Mike Walker.

Illustration Credits

Leland Klanderman, Cover Art; Lori Lohstoeter, 4-5, 8-11; Diane Greenseid, 6-7, 68-71; Pamela Paparone, 12-27; Mary GrandPré 28-29; Tracy Sabin, 12-13, 28, 33; Paul Dolan, 30-31, 48-49, 106-107, 124-125, 142-143; Lisa Campbell Ernst, 32-47; Julia Vivas, 72-103, 106-107; David McPhail, 108-123; Jose Aruego and Ariane Dewey, 126-141